KRISHNA MOHAN AVANCHA

Performance Marketing Steps

First edition

This book was professionally typeset on Reedsy.
Find out more at reedsy.com

Contents

1

What Is Performance Marketing?

Performance marketing is a type of online advertising where advertisers pay only when a specific action is taken by the target audience. This means that advertisers pay only when a user takes a desired action such as clicking on an ad, filling out a form, subscribing to a newsletter, making a purchase, or downloading an app.

Performance marketing is also known as pay-for-performance marketing or affiliate marketing, and it differs from traditional marketing methods such as billboards, TV ads, or radio commercials, where advertisers pay upfront for ad space or airtime regardless of the impact on their business.

The key concept behind performance marketing is that advertisers only pay for the results they get. This allows them to track and measure the success of their campaigns in real-time and optimize their strategies accordingly. Performance marketing is a data-driven approach, and it relies heavily on analytics, tracking, and optimization tools to deliver the best possible results.

Performance marketing can be broken down into three main categories:

1. Affiliate Marketing: In affiliate marketing, advertisers partner with publishers or affiliates who promote their products or services on their websites, social media platforms, or email lists. The affiliate earns a commission for every sale or lead generated through their referral link.
2. Pay-Per-Click Advertising: In pay-per-click advertising, advertisers bid

on keywords relevant to their target audience, and their ads are displayed on search engines or other websites. Advertisers pay a fee each time a user clicks on their ad.

3. Display Advertising: In display advertising, advertisers create visual ads in various formats such as banner ads, pop-ups, or video ads, and these ads are displayed on relevant websites or social media platforms. Advertisers pay a fee for each impression or click generated by their ads.

The benefits of performance marketing are numerous. Firstly, it is a cost-effective approach, as advertisers only pay for the results they get. Secondly, it provides a high level of transparency and accountability, as advertisers can track the performance of their campaigns in real-time and adjust their strategies accordingly. Finally, performance marketing allows advertisers to target specific audiences and reach them at the right time and place, increasing the chances of conversions and sales.

In conclusion, performance marketing is a powerful tool that allows advertisers to optimize their online advertising efforts and achieve their business goals more efficiently. With its data-driven approach, transparency, and flexibility, performance marketing is becoming increasingly popular among businesses of all sizes and industries, and it is expected to continue growing in the future.

Why to do performance marketing?

Performance marketing has become increasingly important in recent years, and for good reason. Here are some key reasons why performance marketing is essential for businesses:

1. Cost-effective: Performance marketing is a cost-effective approach, as advertisers only pay for the results they get. Unlike traditional advertising methods where advertisers pay upfront for ad space or airtime regardless of the impact on their business, performance marketing allows advertisers to pay only when a specific action is taken by the target

audience. This means that advertisers can optimize their budgets and achieve better returns on investment.

2. Measurable results: Performance marketing allows advertisers to track and measure the success of their campaigns in real-time. By using analytics, tracking, and optimization tools, advertisers can monitor the performance of their campaigns and adjust their strategies accordingly. This level of transparency and accountability provides advertisers with insights into the effectiveness of their campaigns and helps them make data-driven decisions.

3. Targeted audience: Performance marketing enables advertisers to reach specific audiences and target them at the right time and place. By using audience targeting tools, advertisers can identify their ideal customers based on factors such as demographics, interests, behavior, and location. This allows advertisers to deliver personalized and relevant messages to their target audience, increasing the chances of conversions and sales.

4. Flexibility: Performance marketing provides advertisers with a high degree of flexibility. Advertisers can adjust their campaigns in real-time based on the performance of their ads. They can change their targeting, messaging, and creative elements to optimize their campaigns and achieve better results. This flexibility allows advertisers to stay ahead of the competition and adapt to changing market conditions.

5. Scalability: Performance marketing is a scalable approach. Advertisers can start small and test their campaigns with a limited budget, and then scale up their efforts as they see positive results. This allows businesses of all sizes to benefit from performance marketing, whether they are startups or large corporations.

In conclusion, performance marketing is a powerful tool that allows advertisers to optimize their online advertising efforts and achieve their business goals more efficiently. With its cost-effectiveness, measurability, targeted audience, flexibility, and scalability, performance marketing has become a critical component of modern marketing strategies. By embracing performance marketing, businesses can stay ahead of the competition and achieve better results in the long run.

2

How is Performance Marketing Different?

P erformance marketing is a type of digital marketing where advertisers only pay for specific actions that have been completed by the audience, such as making a purchase, filling out a form, or downloading an app. Unlike traditional advertising where advertisers pay for the placement of their ads without any guarantee of performance, performance marketing focuses on results and accountability.

One of the main differences between performance marketing and traditional advertising is the pricing model. Performance marketing uses a pay-for-performance model, where advertisers only pay when a specific action is completed by the audience. This means that advertisers have more control over their marketing budget and can measure the success of their campaigns more accurately. In contrast, traditional advertising uses a pay-per-impression or pay-per-click model, where advertisers pay for ad placement regardless of whether or not the audience takes any action.

Another key difference between performance marketing and traditional advertising is the level of targeting and personalization that is possible. Performance marketing relies heavily on data and analytics to target specific audiences based on their behavior, interests, and demographics. This means that performance marketing campaigns can be highly personalized and relevant to the individual user. In contrast, traditional advertising tends to rely on more broad-based targeting, such as demographics or location, which may not be as effective in reaching specific audiences.

Performance marketing also places a strong emphasis on testing and optimization. Advertisers constantly test different ad formats, placements, and messaging to find what works best for their audience. This ongoing optimization helps to maximize the ROI of performance marketing campaigns and ensures that advertisers are only paying for actions that are most valuable to their business.

Finally, performance marketing is highly measurable and transparent. Advertisers have access to real-time data on the performance of their campaigns and can make changes and optimizations quickly based on that data. This level of transparency and accountability is not always present in traditional advertising, where advertisers may not have as much insight into the performance of their campaigns.

In summary, performance marketing is different from traditional advertising in its pricing model, level of targeting and personalization, emphasis on testing and optimization, and level of transparency and accountability. By focusing on results and data-driven decision making, performance marketing can be an effective way for businesses to drive growth and maximize their marketing ROI.

How is performance marketing helpful?

Performance marketing is a highly effective way for businesses to drive growth and maximize their marketing ROI. Here are some of the ways in which performance marketing can be helpful:

1. Cost-Effective: Performance marketing is based on a pay-for-performance model, meaning that advertisers only pay when a specific action is completed by the audience. This means that advertisers have more control over their marketing budget and can optimize their spend to focus on the most valuable actions, such as purchases or lead generation. By only paying for results, performance marketing can be a highly cost-effective way to reach and engage with potential customers.

2. Highly Targeted: Performance marketing relies heavily on data and analytics to target specific audiences based on their behavior, interests, and demographics. This means that performance marketing campaigns can be highly personalized and relevant to the individual user. By targeting the right audience with the right message, businesses can increase the likelihood of conversion and maximize the ROI of their marketing spend.

3. Measurable and Transparent: Performance marketing is highly measurable and transparent. Advertisers have access to real-time data on the performance of their campaigns and can make changes and optimizations quickly based on that data. This level of transparency and accountability is not always present in traditional advertising, where advertisers may not have as much insight into the performance of their campaigns. By having access to data and analytics, businesses can make informed decisions about where to allocate their marketing spend and optimize their campaigns for maximum impact.

4. Testing and Optimization: Performance marketing places a strong emphasis on testing and optimization. Advertisers constantly test different ad formats, placements, and messaging to find what works best for their audience. This ongoing optimization helps to maximize the ROI of performance marketing campaigns and ensures that advertisers are only paying for actions that are most valuable to their business.

5. Scalability: Performance marketing can be highly scalable. Advertisers can start small with a targeted campaign and then gradually expand as they see positive results. By scaling their campaigns in a controlled way, businesses can manage their marketing spend and avoid wasting money on campaigns that are not delivering results.

In summary, performance marketing can be highly beneficial for businesses looking to drive growth and maximize their marketing ROI. By focusing on results, targeting the right audience, using data and analytics to inform decision making, and constantly testing and optimizing campaigns, businesses can increase the effectiveness of their marketing efforts and achieve their business goals more effectively.

3

Performance marketing vs brand marketing

P erformance marketing and brand marketing are two different marketing strategies that businesses use to achieve different goals. While brand marketing focuses on building a brand image and creating a long-term emotional connection with the audience, performance marketing focuses on generating immediate and measurable results.

Performance Marketing:

Performance marketing is a data-driven marketing strategy that uses digital channels such as search engines, social media, and display advertising to drive specific actions, such as clicks, conversions, and sales. The key objective of performance marketing is to drive direct response from the target audience and to measure the success of the campaign through specific KPIs (key performance indicators).

The primary advantage of performance marketing is its ability to deliver quick and measurable results. With performance marketing, businesses can target specific audience segments, track the performance of their campaigns, and optimize their marketing strategies based on the data. This allows businesses to identify what works and what doesn't and to adjust their tactics accordingly.

Brand Marketing:

Brand marketing is a long-term strategy that aims to create a strong brand identity, build trust and credibility with the audience, and establish an emotional connection with the customers. Brand marketing is not just about selling products; it's about creating a brand that customers love and trust.

The primary goal of brand marketing is to create awareness and recognition for the brand, rather than to drive immediate conversions or sales. Brand marketing campaigns often focus on storytelling, creating a unique brand personality, and building a loyal customer base.

The primary advantage of brand marketing is that it creates a lasting impact on the audience. A strong brand identity can help a business stand out from the competition, increase customer loyalty, and even command premium prices for its products or services.

Key Differences:

1. Objective: The primary objective of performance marketing is to drive immediate results, such as clicks, conversions, and sales, while the primary objective of brand marketing is to create awareness and recognition for the brand and to build long-term emotional connections with the audience.

2. Metrics: Performance marketing relies on specific KPIs, such as cost-per-click (CPC), cost-per-acquisition (CPA), and return on ad spend (ROAS), to measure the success of the campaign, while brand marketing relies on more qualitative metrics, such as brand awareness, brand loyalty, and brand perception.

3. Timing: Performance marketing campaigns are usually short-term and tactical, while brand marketing campaigns are usually long-term and strategic.

4. Targeting: Performance marketing is highly targeted, focusing on specific audience segments that are most likely to convert, while brand marketing aims to create a brand image that appeals to a broad audience.

In conclusion, performance marketing and brand marketing are two different marketing strategies that businesses can use to achieve different goals. While performance marketing focuses on delivering immediate results, brand marketing focuses on building a strong brand identity and creating an emotional connection with the audience.

Differences between performance marketing and personal branding

Performance marketing and personal branding are two distinct marketing strategies that businesses and individuals use to achieve their marketing objectives. Although there are some similarities between the two strategies, they differ in terms of their goals, target audience, methods, and outcomes.

Performance marketing is a marketing strategy that aims to increase the revenue of a business by driving specific actions, such as clicks, conversions, or sales. The primary objective of performance marketing is to generate measurable results, such as return on investment (ROI) or cost per acquisition (CPA). Performance marketing is highly data-driven, and marketers use various techniques, such as search engine optimization (SEO), search engine marketing (SEM), affiliate marketing, and email marketing, to achieve their goals.

On the other hand, personal branding is a marketing strategy that aims to build a unique and recognizable image of an individual, rather than a product or service. The primary objective of personal branding is to establish a personal connection with the target audience and create a positive perception of the individual's skills, values, and expertise. Personal branding is highly focused on building relationships and trust, and the methods used to achieve this goal may include social media, blogging, public speaking, and networking.

One of the key differences between performance marketing and personal branding is their target audience. Performance marketing is aimed at a broader audience, including potential customers who are already interested in the product or service. Personal branding, on the other hand, is focused on building relationships with a specific audience, such as a niche group of professionals, customers, or followers.

Another difference between the two marketing strategies is their methods. Performance marketing relies on data-driven techniques that can be easily measured and optimized. Personal branding, on the other hand, is based on more subjective factors, such as personality, authenticity, and storytelling. Personal branding requires more creativity and a unique voice to stand out from the competition.

Finally, the outcomes of performance marketing and personal branding differ as well. Performance marketing aims to increase revenue, improve ROI, and reduce CPA. Personal branding, on the other hand, focuses on building trust, credibility, and a strong reputation, which can lead to more opportunities, such as partnerships, collaborations, and career advancement.

In conclusion, performance marketing and personal branding are two distinct marketing strategies that serve different purposes and use different methods to achieve their goals. While performance marketing is focused on driving measurable results, personal branding is more focused on building relationships and establishing a unique identity. Depending on the marketing objectives, businesses and individuals may choose to use one or both of these strategies to achieve their goals.

4

Performance marketing vs on-page or off-page SEO

erformance marketing and on-page/off-page SEO are two distinct digital marketing strategies that focus on different aspects of optimizing a website for higher visibility, traffic, and conversions. Here is a detailed comparison of performance marketing vs. on-page/off-page SEO:

Performance Marketing:

Performance marketing refers to a set of digital marketing strategies that aim to generate measurable results in terms of conversions, sales, and revenue. The goal of performance marketing is to deliver a return on investment (ROI) by driving relevant traffic to a website, engaging users with compelling content, and persuading them to take a desired action, such as making a purchase, filling out a form, or subscribing to a newsletter.

Some of the common performance marketing tactics include:

1. Pay-per-click (PPC) advertising: This involves placing targeted ads on search engines, social media platforms, or other websites and paying only when users click on the ad.
2. Affiliate marketing: This involves partnering with other websites or individuals to promote products or services in exchange for a

commission on sales.

3. Email marketing: This involves sending targeted emails to a list of subscribers to promote products or services, offer discounts or deals, or provide valuable content.

4. Retargeting: This involves displaying ads to users who have previously visited a website or interacted with a brand but did not convert.

Performance marketing can be highly effective in driving traffic and conversions for a website, as it allows businesses to target specific audiences and measure the impact of their campaigns. However, it can also be costly and competitive, as advertisers bid against each other for the same keywords and placements.

On-page SEO:

On-page SEO refers to the optimization of website content and structure to improve its ranking and visibility on search engines. The goal of on-page SEO is to make a website more relevant, authoritative, and user-friendly, by using targeted keywords, optimizing meta tags, headings, and images, improving site speed and mobile responsiveness, and creating high-quality content that meets the user's search intent.

Some of the common on-page SEO tactics include:

1. Keyword research and optimization: This involves identifying relevant keywords and incorporating them into the website's content, meta tags, headings, and alt text.

2. Content creation: This involves creating high-quality, relevant, and engaging content that meets the user's search intent and provides value to the reader.

3. Site structure and navigation: This involves organizing the website's pages, creating a clear hierarchy, and optimizing the URL structure to make it easy for users and search engines to navigate.

4. Mobile optimization: This involves ensuring that the website is optimized for mobile devices, with fast loading times, easy navigation, and a responsive design.

On-page SEO is a critical component of any digital marketing strategy, as it helps websites rank higher on search engine results pages (SERPs) and attract more organic traffic. However, it can take time to see results, and it requires ongoing optimization and maintenance to stay competitive.

Off-page SEO:

Off-page SEO refers to the optimization of external factors that influence a website's ranking and visibility on search engines. The goal of off-page SEO is to increase the website's authority, credibility, and popularity by building high-quality backlinks from other relevant and trustworthy websites, engaging with users on social media, and creating brand awareness through PR and outreach activities.

Some of the common off-page SEO tactics include:

1. Link building: This involves acquiring high-quality backlinks from other websites, directories, and social media platforms, which signal to search engines that the website is authoritative and trustworthy.
2. Social media marketing: This involves creating and sharing engaging content on social media platforms to increase brand awareness, drive traffic to the website, and engage with users.
3. PR and outreach: This involves reaching out to journalists, bloggers, and influencers

Difference between performance marketing and paid ads

Performance marketing and paid advertising are both types of online marketing that aim to drive traffic to a website, generate leads, and increase sales. However, there are some key differences between the two:

1. Goal: The main goal of paid advertising is to increase brand awareness and attract new customers to a website. Performance marketing, on the other hand, focuses on driving specific actions, such as generating leads or making sales.
2. Payment: In paid advertising, advertisers pay for ad space on a website

or social media platform. In performance marketing, advertisers pay only when a specific action, such as a sale or a lead, is generated.

3. Metrics: The success of paid advertising is measured by metrics such as impressions, clicks, and click-through rates. Performance marketing, on the other hand, is measured by metrics such as cost per lead, cost per sale, and return on investment.

4. Approach: Paid advertising typically involves creating a campaign with a set budget and targeting specific demographics or interests. Performance marketing, on the other hand, focuses on creating targeted campaigns that are designed to generate specific actions.

In summary, paid advertising is focused on generating brand awareness and attracting new customers, while performance marketing is focused on driving specific actions and measuring the success of those actions.

Benefits of performance marketing

Performance marketing is a type of marketing strategy that focuses on achieving specific, measurable goals. The primary objective of performance marketing is to drive user engagement, increase website traffic, generate leads, or boost sales. Performance marketing allows marketers to measure the success of their campaigns accurately, making it a highly effective strategy for businesses of all sizes.

There are several benefits of performing performance marketing. Here are some of the key advantages:

1. Measurable Results: Performance marketing campaigns are designed to achieve specific goals, such as generating leads or driving sales. This means that the success of the campaign can be accurately measured, allowing marketers to determine the return on investment (ROI) of their campaigns. With measurable results, businesses can make data-driven decisions, optimize their campaigns and allocate resources effectively.

2. Cost-Effective: Performance marketing is cost-effective, as advertisers

only pay for the desired outcome. For example, if a campaign is designed to generate leads, the advertiser only pays for the leads generated. This ensures that the budget is spent efficiently, as there is no wasted spend on ineffective campaigns.

3. Targeted Approach: Performance marketing allows businesses to target their desired audience more accurately. By analyzing data such as demographics, interests, and behaviors, businesses can identify the ideal audience for their campaigns. This targeted approach ensures that the right message is delivered to the right audience, resulting in higher engagement and conversion rates.

4. Flexible Campaigns: Performance marketing campaigns are flexible, meaning they can be adapted quickly based on the results. By analyzing the campaign data, businesses can identify areas that need improvement and make changes accordingly. This allows businesses to optimize their campaigns continuously and maximize their results.

5. Brand Awareness: Performance marketing campaigns can also help businesses increase their brand awareness. By targeting the right audience, businesses can introduce their brand to new customers, which can lead to increased engagement and loyalty. As customers become more familiar with the brand, they are more likely to make a purchase or recommend the brand to others.

In conclusion, performance marketing is an effective and cost-efficient marketing strategy that offers several benefits to businesses. By measuring the success of campaigns, targeting the right audience, and making data-driven decisions, businesses can optimize their campaigns and achieve their desired outcomes.

5

Performance marketing vs programmatic marketing

P erformance marketing and programmatic marketing are two important marketing strategies that have emerged in recent years. Both approaches have their own unique features and benefits, and understanding the differences between them can help businesses make more informed decisions about their marketing strategies.

Performance marketing is a type of marketing that focuses on driving specific actions or outcomes, such as clicks, leads, sales, or downloads. This approach is highly targeted, measurable, and accountable, and it often relies on data-driven insights to optimize campaigns for better results. Performance marketing can include a variety of channels and tactics, such as paid search, display advertising, affiliate marketing, email marketing, and social media advertising.

The main advantage of performance marketing is that it allows businesses to track and measure the effectiveness of their campaigns in real-time, and adjust them based on performance data. This means that businesses can optimize their marketing budgets and maximize their return on investment (ROI) by focusing on the channels and tactics that deliver the best results. Performance marketing is also highly scalable, as businesses can easily adjust their budgets and targeting parameters to reach more or fewer potential customers.

Programmatic marketing, on the other hand, is a type of marketing that uses automated technology to buy and optimize digital ad inventory in real-time. Programmatic marketing relies on data-driven insights and algorithms to identify the best ad placements, audiences, and messaging for each campaign. This approach allows businesses to target their ads more precisely and efficiently, and it can help reduce waste and improve ROI.

Programmatic marketing can include a variety of channels and tactics, such as display advertising, video advertising, mobile advertising, and social media advertising. One of the key benefits of programmatic marketing is that it allows businesses to reach their target audiences across multiple devices and channels, including desktop, mobile, and connected TV. This means that businesses can deliver a more cohesive and personalized message to their customers, and increase the likelihood of conversions.

While performance marketing and programmatic marketing share some similarities, they also have some important differences. Performance marketing is focused on driving specific outcomes, while programmatic marketing is focused on using technology to optimize ad delivery and targeting. Performance marketing is highly measurable and accountable, while programmatic marketing is highly automated and efficient. Both approaches can be effective for businesses, depending on their goals, budgets, and target audiences.

Needed performance marketing skillset

Performance marketing requires a unique set of skills that combine creativity, analytical thinking, and technical expertise. To succeed in this field, professionals must have a deep understanding of digital marketing channels, data analysis, and customer behavior. Here are some of the key skills required to excel in performance marketing:

1. Analytics: Performance marketers must have strong analytical skills to be able to measure and optimize the effectiveness of their campaigns.

This includes being able to track metrics such as click-through rates, conversion rates, and cost per acquisition, and using tools like Google Analytics, Adobe Analytics, or other marketing analytics platforms to analyze campaign data and identify opportunities for improvement.

2. Marketing Automation: Performance marketing relies heavily on marketing automation tools such as Google Ads, Facebook Ads, LinkedIn Ads, and other digital advertising platforms to create, launch, and manage campaigns. Therefore, proficiency in these tools is essential to optimize campaign results.

3. Digital Advertising: A solid understanding of digital advertising channels such as PPC, display advertising, social media advertising, and affiliate marketing is necessary. This includes knowledge of how these channels work, their targeting options, and how to create compelling ad copy that will drive conversions.

4. Search Engine Optimization (SEO): SEO is an essential component of performance marketing as it helps businesses to get organic traffic and rank higher in search engine results. Understanding how to research keywords, create content, and optimize websites for search engines is crucial for success in this field.

5. Data Analysis: Performance marketers need to be able to analyze data from multiple sources to identify trends, insights and make decisions about campaigns. This involves using tools such as Excel, Google Sheets, or other data analysis software to create reports, dashboards, and other data visualization tools that will help them identify patterns and trends that can be used to make informed decisions.

6. Project Management: Performance marketing campaigns can be complex, requiring coordination between multiple teams, platforms, and technologies. As a result, strong project management skills are essential to ensure that campaigns are executed on time, within budget, and to the highest quality standards.

7. Creative Thinking: Performance marketing requires creative thinking to come up with new and innovative ideas for campaigns that will capture the attention of potential customers. This includes developing

compelling ad copy, creating eye-catching visuals, and using storytelling techniques to engage audiences.

In conclusion, a successful performance marketer must be skilled in data analysis, marketing automation, digital advertising, SEO, project management, and creative thinking. By having these skills, performance marketers can create, launch, and optimize campaigns that drive measurable results for businesses.

6

How to Measure Performance Marketing?

Performance marketing is a type of digital marketing that focuses on driving specific actions, such as clicks, leads, sales, or other desired outcomes. Unlike traditional advertising, which is often measured by impressions or reach, performance marketing is all about results. Therefore, it's crucial to measure the performance of your campaigns accurately to ensure that you're achieving your business goals.

Here are the steps to measure the performance of your performance marketing campaigns:

1. Define your key performance indicators (KPIs): Before you start measuring anything, you need to identify the metrics that matter most to your business. What do you want to achieve with your performance marketing campaigns? Is it sales, leads, website traffic, or something else? Once you've identified your KPIs, you can use them as a benchmark for your campaigns' success.

2. Set up tracking: Once you've identified your KPIs, you need to set up tracking to measure your campaigns' performance accurately. There are many tracking tools available, such as Google Analytics, Facebook Pixel, and other third-party tracking solutions. These tools allow you to track user behavior on your website or app, measure conversions, and track other relevant metrics.

3. Analyze your data: Once you've collected enough data, it's time to analyze it to see how your campaigns are performing. You can use data visualization tools such as Google Data Studio or Tableau to create reports that show your performance metrics over time. By analyzing your data, you can identify trends, patterns, and opportunities for optimization.

4. Optimize your campaigns: Once you've analyzed your data, you can identify areas of your campaigns that need optimization. This might include changing ad creatives, adjusting targeting, or tweaking your landing pages. By making these changes, you can improve your campaigns' performance and achieve better results.

5. Repeat the process: Performance marketing is an iterative process, so you need to repeat these steps continuously to improve your campaigns' performance over time. By constantly measuring, analyzing, and optimizing your campaigns, you can achieve your business goals more effectively.

In conclusion, measuring the performance of your performance marketing campaigns is crucial to achieving your business goals. By defining your KPIs, setting up tracking, analyzing your data, optimizing your campaigns, and repeating the process, you can improve your campaigns' performance over time and achieve better results.

Who should judge a performance marketing strategy

The right judge for performance marketing done correctly is typically the business or organization that has set the goals for the campaign. They are the ones who can determine if the campaign has achieved the desired results and if it was successful in meeting their business objectives.

In addition, the performance marketing team or agency responsible for executing the campaign can also be a judge of its success. They are the ones who have the expertise to measure and analyze campaign data and make optimization recommendations to improve the campaign's performance.

Other stakeholders, such as customers or users, can also provide valuable feedback on the effectiveness of the campaign. This feedback can come in the form of customer reviews, feedback forms, or social media comments.

Ultimately, the judge of performance marketing done correctly should be based on whether the campaign has achieved its goals, whether it has generated a positive return on investment (ROI), and whether it has provided value to the target audience.

7

The Top measuring terms for Performance Marketing: CPM

Performance marketing is a digital marketing strategy that focuses on driving measurable results such as clicks, conversions, and sales. Measuring the effectiveness of performance marketing campaigns is crucial to understanding their impact and optimizing them for better results. In this regard, there are several key performance indicators (KPIs) that marketers use to measure the success of their campaigns. One such KPI is CPM.

CPM, or cost per mille, is a metric that measures the cost of reaching one thousand (mille) impressions of an ad. This metric is commonly used in display advertising campaigns, where advertisers pay a fee to have their ads displayed on various websites or social media platforms. CPM is calculated by dividing the total cost of the campaign by the number of impressions, then multiplying the result by 1000.

For example, if an advertiser runs a display advertising campaign that costs $10,000 and generates 1 million impressions, the CPM would be calculated as follows:

CPM = ($10,000 / 1,000,000) x 1000 = $10

This means that the advertiser is paying $10 for every 1000 impressions of their ad.

CPM is an important metric for measuring the efficiency of display advertising campaigns. It allows advertisers to compare the cost of running ads across different websites or platforms and determine which ones offer the best value for their money. Additionally, CPM can be used to optimize campaigns by identifying which ads and placements are generating the most impressions at the lowest cost.

However, it's worth noting that CPM is not always the best metric for measuring the effectiveness of performance marketing campaigns. While it may be useful for campaigns focused on increasing brand awareness or generating traffic, it may not provide meaningful insights for campaigns focused on driving conversions or sales. In these cases, metrics such as cost per click (CPC) or cost per acquisition (CPA) may be more relevant.

In conclusion, CPM is a key performance indicator for measuring the efficiency of display advertising campaigns. It allows marketers to compare the cost of running ads across different websites or platforms and optimize campaigns for better results. However, it's important to consider other metrics alongside CPM to get a complete picture of campaign effectiveness.

Why CPM would be a wrong metrics to measure

Measuring CPM alone may not be the best way to determine the effectiveness of a performance marketing campaign focused on gaining leads. While CPM can provide insights into the cost of generating impressions, it doesn't necessarily correlate with the number or quality of leads generated.

Here are some reasons why measuring CPM alone may be wrong when the intended KPI for the strategy is to gain leads:

1. CPM does not measure engagement: While impressions are an important part of the lead generation process, they don't necessarily mean that a user has engaged with the ad. Measuring engagement metrics such as click-through rate (CTR) or time spent on site can provide a better indication of whether users are interacting with the ad and moving towards becoming a lead.

2. CPM doesn't measure the quality of impressions: CPM only measures the cost of generating impressions, but it doesn't differentiate between high-quality and low-quality impressions. For example, an ad displayed on a website that is not relevant to the target audience may generate impressions, but it may not generate quality leads. Measuring metrics such as conversion rate or cost per lead (CPL) can help determine the quality of impressions generated by the campaign.

3. CPM doesn't measure the cost-effectiveness of the campaign: While CPM can provide insights into the cost of generating impressions, it doesn't necessarily indicate whether the campaign is cost-effective in generating leads. A campaign that generates a high number of impressions at a low cost may not necessarily generate quality leads. Measuring metrics such as CPL or return on ad spend (ROAS) can help determine whether the campaign is cost-effective in generating leads.

4. CPM doesn't provide insights into the lead generation process: Measuring CPM alone doesn't provide insights into the lead generation process. To understand how leads are generated, marketers need to measure metrics such as lead conversion rate, lead quality, and cost per lead. By understanding the lead generation process, marketers can optimize their campaigns to generate higher-quality leads at a lower cost.

In conclusion, while measuring CPM is important for display advertising campaigns focused on increasing brand awareness or generating traffic, it may not provide meaningful insights for campaigns focused on gaining leads. To measure the effectiveness of lead generation campaigns, marketers should consider metrics such as engagement, lead quality, cost-effectiveness, and the lead generation process. By measuring these metrics, marketers can optimize their campaigns to generate higher-quality leads at a lower cost.

8

The Top measuring terms for Performance Marketing: CPC

Performance marketing is a type of marketing that focuses on generating measurable results based on specific actions taken by customers. One of the most important measures of performance marketing is cost per click (CPC). In this answer, we'll explore what CPC is, how it's calculated, and why it's such an important metric for measuring the success of performance marketing campaigns.

What is CPC?

CPC stands for cost per click. It is a measure of how much money an advertiser pays for each click that a user makes on an advertisement. CPC is used in online advertising platforms like Google Ads, Facebook Ads, and others, where advertisers bid for ad placements based on specific keywords or target audiences. When a user clicks on an ad, the advertiser pays the platform a certain amount of money, and the user is directed to the advertiser's website or landing page.

How is CPC calculated?

The CPC formula is relatively straightforward: it is the total cost of a campaign divided by the number of clicks generated. For example, if an advertiser spends $100 on a campaign and generates 100 clicks, the CPC would be $1.

CPC can also be calculated at the ad group or keyword level. In this case, the formula would be the total cost of the ad group or keyword divided by the number of clicks generated by that ad group or keyword.

Why is CPC important in performance marketing?

CPC is an important metric in performance marketing because it directly ties advertising spend to user engagement. Unlike traditional advertising methods like television or radio, where it's difficult to track how many people saw or heard an ad and took action, performance marketing allows advertisers to measure how many users clicked on an ad and took a desired action, such as making a purchase or filling out a form.

CPC is also important because it allows advertisers to optimize their campaigns for maximum return on investment (ROI). By monitoring CPC, advertisers can see which keywords and ad groups are generating the most clicks and conversions and adjust their bids and targeting accordingly. This helps to ensure that advertising spend is being used effectively and efficiently.

In addition, CPC can be used to compare the performance of different advertising platforms, campaigns, and keywords. By analyzing CPC across multiple campaigns, advertisers can identify which platforms and strategies are working best and allocate their budget accordingly.

Conclusion

CPC is a critical metric for measuring the success of performance marketing campaigns. By understanding how it's calculated and using it to optimize ad spend and targeting, advertisers can achieve better ROI and drive more engagement and conversions. As such, it's important for performance marketers to track CPC closely and use it as one of their key measures of success.

When would CPC be a wrong metric to track

While CPC is a widely used metric for performance marketing, some argue that it is not always the most appropriate or accurate measure of success. Here are a few reasons why CPC might be considered a wrong metric for performance marketing:

1. It doesn't account for conversions: While CPC is a measure of how much it costs to generate a click, it doesn't take into account whether that click actually leads to a conversion, such as a sale or a sign-up. For example, an advertiser might generate a lot of clicks with a low CPC, but if those clicks don't lead to any conversions, then the campaign is not really successful.

2. It doesn't consider the lifetime value of a customer: CPC is focused on the immediate cost of generating a click, but it doesn't account for the potential long-term value of a customer. For example, if an advertiser spends more on CPC to acquire a customer who will make repeat purchases in the future, that investment might be worth it in the long run, even if the immediate CPC is higher.

3. It doesn't reflect the quality of traffic: Not all clicks are created equal, and CPC doesn't distinguish between clicks that are more likely to result in a conversion versus clicks that are less likely to convert. For example, if an advertiser is targeting a broad audience with a low CPC, they might generate a lot of clicks from people who are not actually interested in their product or service. This can lead to a high bounce rate and a low conversion rate, even though the CPC is low.

4. It doesn't consider other factors that contribute to success: While CPC is an important metric, it is not the only factor that contributes to the success of a performance marketing campaign. Other factors, such as ad copy, landing page design, targeting, and timing, can also have a significant impact on campaign performance.

In conclusion, while CPC is a widely used metric for performance marketing, it is not always the most appropriate or accurate measure of success. Advertisers should consider other metrics, such as conversion rate, customer lifetime value, and quality of traffic, in addition to CPC when evaluating the success of their campaigns. Ultimately, the most important measure of success will depend on the specific goals and objectives of the campaign.

9

The Top measuring terms for Performance Marketing: CPA

P erformance marketing is a form of digital advertising that focuses on driving measurable results and outcomes, such as clicks, leads, sales, and other actions that can be directly attributed to advertising campaigns. Unlike traditional advertising, performance marketing is highly data-driven and relies on a variety of key performance indicators (KPIs) to measure and optimize campaign performance. One of the most important KPIs in performance marketing is CPA, or cost per acquisition. In this article, we'll take a closer look at CPA and its importance in measuring the success of performance marketing campaigns.

CPA Definition

Cost per acquisition (CPA) is a metric that measures the cost of acquiring a new customer or lead through a specific marketing campaign or channel. CPA is calculated by dividing the total cost of the campaign by the number of new customers or leads generated during that campaign. For example, if you spent $1,000 on a Facebook ad campaign and generated 100 new customers, your CPA would be $10.

Why CPA Matters in Performance Marketing

CPA is a critical metric in performance marketing because it helps advertisers understand the true cost of acquiring new customers or leads. By tracking CPA, advertisers can identify which campaigns and channels are driving the most cost-effective results and adjust their strategies accordingly. CPA also helps advertisers set realistic campaign goals and budgets, as they can calculate the expected CPA for each campaign based on past performance.

CPA vs. Other Performance Marketing Metrics

CPA is just one of several performance marketing metrics that advertisers use to track and optimize campaign performance. Other common metrics include:

1. Cost per click (CPC): This measures the cost of each click on an ad. CPC is often used in paid search advertising and social media advertising.
2. Conversion rate: This measures the percentage of website visitors who take a desired action, such as making a purchase or filling out a lead form.
3. Return on ad spend (ROAS): This measures the revenue generated for every dollar spent on advertising. ROAS is a more comprehensive metric than CPA, as it takes into account both the cost of advertising and the revenue generated from that advertising.
4. Click-through rate (CTR): This measures the percentage of people who click on an ad after seeing it. CTR is often used in display advertising and social media advertising.

While each of these metrics is important, CPA is unique in that it directly measures the cost of acquiring new customers or leads. As a result, CPA is often used as a primary KPI in performance marketing campaigns.

How to Improve CPA

Improving CPA requires a deep understanding of campaign performance and a willingness to test and optimize different strategies. Here are some tips for improving CPA:

1. Target the right audience: Ensure that your ads are reaching the right audience by targeting specific demographics, interests, and behaviors.
2. Use ad retargeting: Retargeting is a technique that involves showing ads

to people who have previously interacted with your brand or website. Retargeting can be highly effective in driving conversions and reducing CPA.

3. Test different ad formats: Experiment with different ad formats, such as video ads, carousel ads, and dynamic ads, to see which ones perform best for your audience.

4. Optimize landing pages: Ensure that your landing pages are optimized for conversions by testing different headlines, images, and calls-to-action.

5. Monitor and adjust bids: Adjust your bids based on campaign performance to ensure that you are bidding the right amount for each click or impression.

Conclusion

CPA is a critical metric in performance marketing that measures the cost of acquiring new customers or leads through specific campaigns or channels. By tracking CPA, advertisers can identify which campaigns are driving the most cost-effective results and adjust their strategies accordingly. To improve CPA, advertisers must have a deep understanding of campaign performance and be willing to test

CPA would be a wrong metric to measure if

While CPA (Cost per Acquisition) is a widely used and effective metric for measuring the success of performance marketing campaigns, there are some scenarios in which it may not be the best metric to use. In this article, we'll take a closer look at when CPA would be a wrong metric and what other metrics may be more appropriate.

1. When the goal is brand awareness

CPA is a metric that measures the cost of acquiring new customers or leads through a specific marketing campaign or channel. If the primary goal of a campaign is to build brand awareness and reach as many people as possible, CPA may not be the best metric to use. In this case, metrics such as reach, impressions, and frequency may be more appropriate.

1. When the sales cycle is long

CPA is most effective when the sales cycle is short and the path to conversion is relatively straightforward. However, if the sales cycle is long and involves multiple touchpoints, it may be more appropriate to use other metrics such as customer lifetime value (CLV) or return on ad spend (ROAS) to measure the success of the campaign.

1. When the campaign involves multiple goals

CPA is a metric that is specific to a single goal, such as acquiring a new customer or lead. If a campaign involves multiple goals, such as both lead generation and sales, CPA may not be the best metric to use. Instead, metrics such as conversion rate, lead-to-sale ratio, and revenue per lead may be more appropriate.

1. When the product or service has a low margin

CPA is a metric that measures the cost of acquiring a new customer or lead. If the product or service being offered has a low profit margin, CPA may not be the best metric to use, as it may not accurately reflect the true value of the customer. In this case, metrics such as CLV or customer acquisition cost (CAC) may be more appropriate.

1. When the campaign involves multiple channels

CPA is a metric that is specific to a single channel or campaign. If a campaign involves multiple channels, such as social media, search advertising, and email marketing, CPA may not be the best metric to use. Instead, metrics such as overall return on investment (ROI) or attribution modeling may be more appropriate.

In conclusion, while CPA is a widely used and effective metric for measuring the success of performance marketing campaigns, it may not be the best metric to use in every scenario. Advertisers should carefully consider their campaign goals and the nature of their product or service before deciding which metrics to use. By selecting the most appropriate metrics, advertisers can ensure that they are measuring the right outcomes and making informed decisions about how to optimize their campaigns.

10

The Top measuring terms for Performance Marketing: LTV

Performance marketing is a form of digital advertising where advertisers only pay for measurable results, such as clicks, leads, or sales. To measure the effectiveness of performance marketing campaigns, advertisers use a range of metrics that allow them to track their return on investment (ROI) and optimize their campaigns for better results. One of the most important metrics used in performance marketing is Lifetime Value (LTV).

Lifetime Value (LTV) is a measure of the total value a customer will bring to a business over the course of their lifetime as a customer. This metric takes into account not only the initial purchase but also the recurring revenue generated from repeat purchases, as well as any additional revenue generated from cross-selling or upselling.

To calculate LTV, you need to know two key pieces of information: the average customer lifespan and the average revenue per customer. The formula for calculating LTV is:

LTV = Average revenue per customer * Customer lifespan

For example, let's say you run an e-commerce store and your average customer spends $50 per purchase and makes five purchases over the course of three years before moving on to a competitor. Your LTV would be:

LTV = $50 * 5 * 3 = $750

This means that the average customer is worth $750 to your business over the course of their lifetime.

LTV is an important metric for performance marketing because it allows advertisers to focus their efforts on acquiring high-value customers who are more likely to generate revenue over the long term. By calculating LTV, advertisers can determine how much they can afford to spend on customer acquisition and retention efforts, such as advertising, promotions, and loyalty programs.

In addition to LTV, there are several other key metrics used in performance marketing:

1. Customer Acquisition Cost (CAC) - This is the cost of acquiring a new customer. To calculate CAC, divide the total cost of your marketing and sales efforts by the number of new customers acquired.
2. Return on Ad Spend (ROAS) - This is a measure of the revenue generated from an advertising campaign compared to the cost of the campaign. To calculate ROAS, divide the revenue generated by the campaign by the cost of the campaign.
3. Click-through Rate (CTR) - This is a measure of how many people click on an ad compared to how many people see the ad. To calculate CTR, divide the number of clicks by the number of impressions.
4. Conversion Rate (CR) - This is a measure of how many people take a desired action (such as making a purchase) compared to how many people visit a website. To calculate CR, divide the number of conversions by the number of visitors.

In conclusion, Lifetime Value (LTV) is a critical metric for measuring the effectiveness of performance marketing campaigns. By calculating LTV, advertisers can determine how much they can afford to spend on acquiring and retaining customers, as well as optimize their campaigns for better long-term results. Additionally, CAC, ROAS, CTR, and CR are other important metrics that can help advertisers track their performance and improve their results over time.

LTV would be a wrong metric to be tracking if

While LTV is a valuable metric for many businesses, there are situations where it may not be the best metric to track. Here are a few scenarios where LTV might not be the best metric to use:

1. Short Customer Lifespan: If your customers have a short lifespan, meaning they only make a few purchases before leaving, then LTV may not be the best metric to use. In this case, focusing on customer acquisition and conversion rates may be more important than LTV, as the revenue generated from each customer may not justify a high acquisition cost.

2. Low Frequency Purchases: If your business sells products or services that are purchased infrequently, such as furniture or home appliances, then LTV may not be the best metric to use. In this case, the time between purchases may be so long that calculating LTV becomes difficult, and focusing on customer satisfaction and loyalty may be more important than LTV.

3. Low-Margin Products: If your business sells products with low margins, such as discounted or low-priced products, then LTV may not be the best metric to use. In this case, the revenue generated from each customer may not justify a high acquisition cost, and focusing on driving volume through lower cost channels may be more important than LTV.

4. High Customer Churn: If your business has a high customer churn rate, meaning customers leave your business quickly after their initial purchase, then LTV may not be the best metric to use. In this case, focusing on customer retention and reducing churn may be more important than LTV, as the value of each customer may be limited by the likelihood that they will leave quickly.

In summary, while LTV is a valuable metric for many businesses, there are situations where it may not be the best metric to use. In these cases, it may be more valuable to focus on other metrics that better reflect the unique characteristics of your business and customer base. By carefully evaluating your business and customer data, you can determine the most appropriate metrics to track and optimize for, ultimately driving better business outcomes.

11

How to Build a Performance Marketing Strategy: Step 1: Establish your campaign goal

erformance marketing is a digital marketing strategy that aims to drive measurable results, such as leads, sales, or website traffic. To build a successful performance marketing strategy, you need to start by establishing your campaign goals. Here are the steps to do that:

Step 1: Establish your campaign goals

The first step in building a performance marketing strategy is to define your campaign goals. Your goals should be specific, measurable, achievable, relevant, and time-bound (SMART). Examples of performance marketing goals include:

- Increase website traffic: If you want to increase the number of visitors to your website, you may want to focus on tactics like search engine optimization (SEO), pay-per-click (PPC) advertising, or social media advertising.
- Generate leads: If you want to generate more leads for your business, you may want to focus on tactics like email marketing, content marketing, or social media advertising.

- Drive sales: If your primary goal is to drive sales, you may want to focus on tactics like retargeting ads, affiliate marketing, or influencer marketing.

When establishing your campaign goals, it's important to consider your budget, timeline, and resources. You should also take into account your target audience and the types of digital channels they are most likely to engage with.

Once you have established your campaign goals, you can begin to develop a strategy that will help you achieve those goals. In the next steps, you will need to define your target audience, select the appropriate digital channels, and create your campaign messaging and creative assets.

Overall, by clearly defining your campaign goals, you can ensure that you are building a performance marketing strategy that is focused on delivering the results you want to achieve.

Detailed steps in performance marketing:

Performance marketing is a data-driven form of marketing that focuses on optimizing campaigns to achieve specific performance goals, such as generating leads, sales, or website traffic. Here are the steps involved in creating and executing a successful performance marketing campaign:

1. Set Clear Goals: The first step in any successful marketing campaign is to set clear and measurable goals. Performance marketing is all about achieving specific performance metrics, so you need to know what you are trying to achieve. For example, you may want to generate a certain number of leads, increase website traffic by a certain percentage, or achieve a certain return on ad spend (ROAS).

2. Identify Your Target Audience: Next, you need to identify your target audience. Who are the people most likely to engage with your ads and convert into customers? You can use data analytics tools to identify your target audience based on demographic, geographic, and psychographic factors.

3. Develop a Marketing Strategy: Once you know your goals and target

audience, you can develop a marketing strategy that will help you achieve those goals. This may include choosing the right marketing channels (such as social media, search engines, or email marketing), creating compelling ad copy and creative, and developing landing pages that are optimized for conversions.

4. Set Up Your Campaign: Once you have a strategy in place, it's time to set up your campaign. This involves setting up your ad accounts, creating ad campaigns, and targeting your ads to your target audience. Make sure to use tracking tools like UTM parameters and conversion tracking pixels to measure the success of your campaigns.

5. Optimize Your Campaign: As your campaign runs, you'll want to continually optimize it to achieve better results. This involves monitoring your campaigns regularly, analyzing your data, and making data-driven decisions about what changes to make to your campaigns. For example, you may need to adjust your targeting, change your ad creative, or adjust your bidding strategies to achieve better results.

6. Measure Your Results: It's important to regularly measure your results to see how your campaign is performing. Use analytics tools to track your performance metrics, such as click-through rate (CTR), conversion rate, and ROAS. Use this data to make informed decisions about how to optimize your campaign further.

7. Refine Your Strategy: Finally, use the data you've gathered to refine your strategy for future campaigns. Identify what worked well and what didn't, and use this information to create even more effective campaigns in the future. By continually refining your strategy, you can improve your performance marketing results over time.

Overall, performance marketing is all about using data to achieve specific performance goals. By setting clear goals, identifying your target audience, developing a marketing strategy, setting up and optimizing your campaigns, measuring your results, and refining your strategy, you can create successful performance marketing campaigns that drive real business results.

12

How to Build a Performance Marketing Strategy: Step 2: Choose your digital channel(s)

C hoosing the right digital channel(s) for your performance marketing strategy is critical to its success. In step 1, you have already identified your target audience, and now it's time to determine where they spend their time online. Once you understand the digital channels that your target audience uses, you can create campaigns that resonate with them and drive results. In this article, we'll discuss the key digital channels to consider when building your performance marketing strategy.

1. Search Engine Marketing (SEM) Search Engine Marketing is a great way to reach your target audience. SEM includes both paid search and organic search. Paid search involves paying for ads to appear at the top of search engine results pages (SERPs) when someone types in a relevant keyword. Organic search involves optimizing your website and content to appear in the non-paid (organic) results. By leveraging SEM, you can reach people who are actively searching for products or services like yours.

2. Social Media Advertising Social media advertising is another effective

way to reach your target audience. Platforms like Facebook, Instagram, Twitter, and LinkedIn allow you to target users based on their interests, behaviors, and demographics. This allows you to create highly targeted ads that are more likely to resonate with your audience. Social media advertising is also relatively inexpensive, making it a great option for businesses with limited budgets.

3. Display Advertising Display advertising involves placing ads on third-party websites, such as news sites or blogs. These ads can be in the form of banners, videos, or other formats. Display advertising allows you to reach a wider audience, but it can be more difficult to target specific users. To make the most of display advertising, consider using retargeting, which involves showing ads to people who have already visited your website.

4. Influencer Marketing Influencer marketing involves partnering with individuals who have a large following on social media. These individuals can help promote your brand and products to their followers, which can increase brand awareness and drive sales. When selecting influencers, it's important to choose individuals whose audience aligns with your target audience. Also, make sure that the influencer's followers are authentic and engaged.

5. Email Marketing Email marketing involves sending promotional emails to your subscribers. This can be an effective way to reach people who have already expressed interest in your brand. By segmenting your email list and creating targeted campaigns, you can ensure that your messages are relevant to your audience. Additionally, email marketing allows you to track metrics like open rates and click-through rates, which can help you optimize your campaigns over time.

6. Affiliate Marketing Affiliate marketing involves partnering with other businesses or individuals to promote your products or services. Affiliates earn a commission for each sale or lead they generate. This can be an effective way to reach new customers and drive sales, but it's important to choose affiliates who align with your brand values and messaging.

In conclusion, choosing the right digital channels for your performance marketing strategy is critical to its success. By understanding where your target audience spends their time online, you can create campaigns that resonate with them and drive results. Consider leveraging a combination of these channels to create a well-rounded strategy that reaches your audience across multiple touchpoints.

steps to choose the digital platform for performance marketing

Choosing the right digital platform for your performance marketing strategy is essential for achieving your business goals. A platform that is popular among your target audience and aligns with your brand values will help you reach a wider audience and generate better results. Here are the steps you can follow to choose the digital platform for your performance marketing strategy:

1. Identify your target audience The first step in choosing a digital platform for your performance marketing strategy is to identify your target audience. Understand who your ideal customers are, their demographics, interests, and behavior. Once you know your target audience, you can identify the platforms they use the most.
2. Research digital platforms Once you have identified your target audience, research the digital platforms that are popular among them. For example, if your target audience consists of young adults, social media platforms like Instagram and TikTok could be ideal. On the other hand, if you are targeting professionals, LinkedIn could be a better option.
3. Analyze platform features After identifying the popular digital platforms, analyze the features they offer. Evaluate if the platform's features align with your business goals and can help you achieve your objectives. For example, if your goal is to generate leads, a platform that offers lead capture forms can be beneficial.
4. Evaluate advertising options Most digital platforms offer advertising options that allow you to target your audience and reach a wider

audience. Evaluate the advertising options of each platform and see if they align with your advertising goals. Consider the advertising formats available, ad targeting options, ad placements, and pricing models.

5. Consider platform suitability for your brand Your brand values and messaging should align with the digital platform you choose for your performance marketing strategy. Evaluate if the platform is suitable for your brand by considering its tone, user-generated content, and user behavior. For example, if your brand is family-oriented, you may not want to advertise on platforms with adult content.

6. Review competitors' platforms Lastly, review the digital platforms your competitors are using for their performance marketing strategy. This will give you an idea of the platforms that are working well for your competitors and help you identify opportunities to differentiate your brand. Consider the platforms your competitors are using and their advertising strategies.

In conclusion, choosing the right digital platform for your performance marketing strategy requires research, analysis, and evaluation. By following these steps, you can identify the platforms that are popular among your target audience, align with your brand values, and offer the features and advertising options that can help you achieve your business goals.

13

How to Build a Performance Marketing Strategy: Step 3: Create and launch the campaign

I n the previous steps, you've set your objectives, identified your target audience, and selected your marketing channels. Now it's time to create and launch your performance marketing campaign. This step requires careful planning and execution to ensure your campaign is successful in achieving your goals.

1. Set your budget: Start by setting a budget for your campaign. This will help you determine how much you can spend on each channel and how much you can invest in creative assets like graphics and videos. Make sure to allocate your budget based on the channels that will yield the highest ROI for your business.

2. Develop your creative assets: Once you've set your budget, you'll need to develop creative assets for your campaign. These can include graphics, videos, and ad copy. Make sure your creative assets are attention-grabbing and aligned with your brand messaging.

3. Define your campaign metrics: To measure the success of your campaign, you'll need to define your campaign metrics. This can include metrics

like click-through rates, conversion rates, and cost per acquisition. Make sure to track your metrics regularly and adjust your campaign strategy accordingly.

4. Launch your campaign: Once you've developed your creative assets and defined your campaign metrics, it's time to launch your campaign. Make sure to launch your campaign across all the channels you've selected. Monitor your campaign closely to ensure everything is running smoothly and adjust your strategy if necessary.

5. Optimize your campaign: Once your campaign is up and running, it's essential to optimize it regularly. This can include adjusting your ad copy, targeting, and creative assets to improve performance. Make sure to monitor your campaign metrics regularly and adjust your strategy as needed.

6. Test and iterate: Finally, it's crucial to test and iterate your campaign continually. This can include A/B testing different ad copy, targeting different audiences, and testing different creative assets. Use the insights gained from your testing to improve your campaign strategy and achieve better results.

By following these steps, you can create and launch a successful performance marketing campaign. Remember to continually monitor and optimize your campaign to achieve the best possible results.

What all needs to be checked before the launch:

Before launching a performance marketing campaign, it's essential to ensure that everything is in place to achieve the best possible results. Here are some key things to check and have in place before launching your campaign:

1. Landing Pages: Ensure that you have dedicated landing pages for each marketing channel you're using. Landing pages should be optimized for conversions and aligned with your ad copy and messaging. Make sure that all links and forms are working correctly.

2. Tracking & Analytics: Set up tracking and analytics to measure the success of your campaign. Make sure that tracking codes are installed correctly on your website and landing pages. This will help you understand your campaign's performance and make data-driven decisions.

3. Ad Copy & Creative Assets: Check that your ad copy and creative assets are finalized and optimized for each channel. Ensure that your ad copy is compelling and aligned with your landing page and messaging. Make sure that all graphics and videos are high-quality and meet the technical requirements of each platform.

4. Targeting & Segmentation: Ensure that your targeting and segmentation are set up correctly. Use data-driven insights to target the right audience for your campaign. Make sure that your audience segments are specific and aligned with your campaign goals.

5. Budget & Bid Management: Make sure that your budget and bid management are in place. Set a budget for each channel and ensure that your bids are optimized for the best possible results. Make sure that you're not overspending on low-performing channels.

6. Testing & Optimization: Check that you have a plan for testing and optimization in place. Set up A/B tests for your ad copy, targeting, and creative assets. Continuously monitor and optimize your campaign to achieve the best possible results.

7. Compliance & Legal Requirements: Ensure that your campaign complies with all legal and regulatory requirements. Check that your ad copy and creative assets are not violating any rules or guidelines. Ensure that you're not using any copyrighted or trademarked content without permission.

By checking these key elements before launching your performance marketing campaign, you can ensure that everything is in place to achieve the best possible results. Remember to monitor and optimize your campaign continuously to achieve your goals.

How to detect performance marketing campaign failure?

Performance marketing campaigns are designed to achieve specific objectives, such as increasing website traffic, generating leads, or boosting sales. However, sometimes campaigns can fail to meet their goals, resulting in poor performance and a low return on investment (ROI). Here are some common signs of performance marketing campaign failure and how to detect them:

1. Low click-through rates (CTR): If your ad is not getting enough clicks, it's a sign that your ad copy or creative assets are not compelling enough to grab the attention of your target audience. You may need to revise your ad copy, optimize your creative assets, or adjust your targeting.

2. High bounce rates: If visitors are leaving your landing pages quickly without taking any action, it's a sign that your landing pages are not aligned with your ad copy or messaging. You may need to revise your landing pages to make them more engaging and relevant to your target audience.

3. Low conversion rates: If visitors are not taking the desired action on your landing pages, such as filling out a form or making a purchase, it's a sign that your landing pages are not optimized for conversions. You may need to revise your landing pages or offer to make them more appealing to your target audience.

4. High cost per acquisition (CPA): If your campaign is costing more per conversion than expected, it's a sign that your targeting, ad copy, or creative assets may not be aligned with your campaign goals. You may need to adjust your targeting, optimize your ad copy or creative assets, or revise your budget and bidding strategy.

5. Poor ROI: If your campaign is not generating a positive return on investment, it's a sign that your campaign is not performing well. You may need to adjust your strategy or pause the campaign if it's not generating the desired results.

To detect performance marketing campaign failure, it's essential to monitor your campaign metrics regularly and track your ROI. Use analytics tools to gain insights into your campaign's performance and adjust your strategy accordingly. By detecting and addressing issues early on, you can optimize your performance marketing campaign to achieve the best possible results.

14

How to Build a Performance Marketing Strategy: Step 4: Measure and optimize your campaign

O nce your performance marketing campaign is up and running, the next step is to measure and optimize its performance. Here are the key steps to do so:

1. Set up tracking and analytics: You need to track the performance of your campaign to optimize it. Set up tracking tools like Google Analytics, Facebook Pixel, or other analytics software to measure metrics like traffic, conversions, and engagement.
2. Define your KPIs: Your key performance indicators (KPIs) are the metrics that you will use to measure the success of your campaign. They will vary depending on your campaign goals, but could include metrics like click-through rates (CTR), conversion rates, cost per acquisition (CPA), and return on investment (ROI).
3. Analyze your data: Once you have collected data from your tracking and analytics tools, it's time to analyze it. Look for patterns and trends in the data, identify what's working and what's not, and identify areas for improvement.

4. Optimize your campaign: Based on your data analysis, make changes to your campaign to improve its performance. This could include tweaking your ad targeting, adjusting your bidding strategy, changing your ad creative, or optimizing your landing pages.

5. Test and iterate: Performance marketing is an iterative process, and you need to constantly test and refine your approach. Test different ad formats, targeting options, and landing page designs to see what works best for your audience. Use A/B testing and other testing methods to measure the impact of your changes.

6. Monitor and adjust: Finally, you need to monitor the performance of your campaign on an ongoing basis and make adjustments as needed. Keep an eye on your KPIs and adjust your strategy as needed to ensure that you are achieving your campaign goals.

In conclusion, measuring and optimizing your campaign is a critical step in building a successful performance marketing strategy. By setting up tracking and analytics, defining your KPIs, analyzing your data, optimizing your campaign, testing and iterating, and monitoring and adjusting, you can ensure that your campaign is delivering the results you need to achieve your business goals.

How to cross verify your metrics and tracking, analytics for performance marketing is set correctly or not?

Cross verifying your metrics and tracking analytics for performance marketing is an essential step to ensure that your data is accurate and reliable. Here are the key steps to follow:

1. Check your tracking tags: The first step is to ensure that your tracking tags are correctly installed on your website and landing pages. Check that your tracking pixels and codes are firing correctly and that they are capturing the right data.

2. Test your tracking: Once your tracking tags are installed, you need to

test them to ensure that they are working correctly. Visit your website or landing page and check that your tracking tools are capturing the correct data, such as page views, clicks, and conversions.

3. Compare data across platforms: If you are using multiple platforms for tracking, such as Google Analytics and Facebook Pixel, you need to compare data across these platforms to ensure consistency. Look for discrepancies in data and identify the source of the issue.

4. Verify your conversion tracking: Conversion tracking is critical for performance marketing, as it allows you to measure the success of your campaigns. Verify that your conversion tracking is set up correctly and that it is capturing all relevant actions, such as form submissions or product purchases.

5. Check your attribution models: Attribution models determine how credit is assigned to different touchpoints in the customer journey. Verify that your attribution model is set up correctly and that it is accurately attributing conversions to the right channels and campaigns.

6. Audit your data: Finally, perform a thorough audit of your data to ensure that it is accurate and reliable. Look for outliers, inconsistencies, and anomalies in your data and investigate the cause of these issues.

By following these steps, you can ensure that your metrics and tracking analytics for performance marketing are set up correctly. This will enable you to make informed decisions based on accurate data, and optimize your campaigns for maximum impact.

Open source solutions for performance marketing:

Performance marketing is a data-driven approach to marketing that focuses on optimizing campaigns for specific key performance indicators (KPIs) such as click-through rates, conversions, and return on investment. While there are many proprietary performance marketing tools available, open-source solutions can offer several advantages, including cost savings, flexibility, and customization options. Here are some of the top open-source solutions for performance marketing:

1. Matomo: Matomo is an open-source web analytics platform that allows you to track website traffic, user behavior, and conversion rates. It offers a range of features including custom dashboards, real-time analytics, and A/B testing.

2. Google Analytics: While not strictly open-source, Google Analytics is a free analytics platform that offers robust tracking and reporting features. It allows you to track website traffic, conversion rates, and user behavior, and offers advanced features such as audience segmentation and funnel visualization.

3. Piwik PRO: Piwik PRO is an enterprise-level web analytics platform that is based on the open-source Matomo software. It offers advanced features such as multi-channel attribution, user-level tracking, and data integration with other marketing tools.

4. Open Web Analytics: Open Web Analytics is a free, open-source web analytics platform that allows you to track website traffic, user behavior, and conversion rates. It offers features such as heatmaps, click-tracking, and real-time analytics.

5. Mautic: Mautic is an open-source marketing automation platform that allows you to automate your email campaigns, landing pages, and lead scoring. It offers a range of features including lead management, A/B testing, and multi-channel campaign management.

6. AdWords Scripts: AdWords Scripts is an open-source scripting platform that allows you to automate your Google AdWords campaigns. It offers features such as bid management, reporting, and budget tracking.

In conclusion, open-source solutions can provide cost-effective and flexible options for performance marketing. By leveraging these tools, you can track and optimize your campaigns for maximum impact and achieve your marketing goals.

15

How to Build a Performance Marketing Strategy: Step 5: Handle potential pitfalls

B uilding a performance marketing strategy can be a complex process, and even the most carefully planned strategies can encounter unexpected obstacles along the way. In this step, we'll discuss some of the potential pitfalls you may face and how to handle them effectively.

1. Poor targeting: One of the most common pitfalls in performance marketing is poor targeting. If you're not targeting the right audience, your campaigns will not perform as well as they could. To avoid this, make sure you have a deep understanding of your target audience and use data to refine your targeting over time.

2. Low-quality traffic: Another common problem is low-quality traffic. If you're not careful, you may end up attracting visitors who are not interested in your products or services. To avoid this, make sure you're using the right keywords and targeting the right audience. You may also want to consider using tools to filter out unwanted traffic.

3. Poor conversion rates: Even if you're attracting the right traffic, you may still struggle with poor conversion rates. There are many reasons why this can happen, including poor website design, confusing messaging, or a lack of trust signals. To address this, make sure your website is

user-friendly, your messaging is clear and compelling, and you're using trust signals such as customer reviews and social proof.

4. Ad fatigue: Over time, your target audience may become fatigued by your ads and stop engaging with them. To avoid this, make sure you're refreshing your ads regularly and testing new creative ideas. You may also want to consider using ad sequencing or retargeting to keep your brand top of mind.

5. Ad fraud: Unfortunately, ad fraud is a significant problem in the performance marketing industry. To protect yourself, make sure you're working with reputable partners and using tools to monitor your campaigns for suspicious activity. You may also want to consider using fraud detection software to help identify and prevent fraudulent activity.

6. Budget constraints: Finally, budget constraints can be a major hurdle in performance marketing. If you're not careful, you may find yourself overspending or not allocating your budget effectively. To avoid this, make sure you have a clear budget in place and are tracking your expenses closely. You may also want to consider using tools to optimize your budget and identify areas where you can cut costs.

In conclusion, building a successful performance marketing strategy requires careful planning and ongoing attention to detail. By anticipating potential pitfalls and taking steps to address them, you can maximize the effectiveness of your campaigns and achieve your marketing goals.

What are some common mistakes to avoid in performance marketing?

Performance marketing is a type of digital marketing that focuses on driving specific actions, such as clicks, sign-ups, or purchases. When done right, performance marketing can be an effective way to drive ROI and grow your business. However, there are several common mistakes that marketers make that can negatively impact the performance of their campaigns. Here are some of the most common mistakes to avoid in performance marketing:

1. Poorly defined goals: One of the most common mistakes in performance marketing is not having clear goals. You need to define specific, measurable, and achievable goals before launching your campaign. This will help you stay focused and ensure that you are driving the right actions.

2. Targeting the wrong audience: Another common mistake in performance marketing is targeting the wrong audience. You need to identify your target audience based on demographics, behavior, and interests. Otherwise, you may end up wasting your budget on people who are not interested in your product or service.

3. Not optimizing your landing pages: Landing pages are an essential part of any performance marketing campaign. If your landing pages are not optimized for conversions, you may lose potential customers. You need to ensure that your landing pages are visually appealing, easy to navigate, and have a clear call-to-action.

4. Poor ad creative: Ad creative plays a critical role in performance marketing. If your ads are not compelling or relevant to your target audience, they may not convert. You need to create ads that are visually appealing, have a clear message, and resonate with your audience.

5. Neglecting data analysis: Data analysis is crucial in performance marketing. If you are not tracking and analyzing your data, you may miss opportunities to optimize your campaigns. You need to track key performance indicators (KPIs) and use data to make data-driven decisions.

6. Not testing enough: A/B testing is an essential part of performance marketing. If you are not testing different ad creative, landing pages, or targeting strategies, you may miss opportunities to improve your performance. You need to test different variables to find what works best for your audience.

7. Overreliance on a single channel: Relying too much on a single channel can be a significant risk in performance marketing. You need to diversify your channels to reach a broader audience and reduce your risk.

In conclusion, performance marketing can be a powerful tool for driving ROI and growing your business. However, to avoid these common mistakes, you need to set clear goals, target the right audience, optimize your landing pages, create compelling ad creative, analyze your data, test different variables, and diversify your channels. By doing so, you can optimize your performance marketing campaigns and achieve better results.

Find the reason for causing your performance marketing failure

If your performance marketing campaign is not delivering the expected results, it can be challenging to pinpoint the exact cause of the failure. However, by systematically reviewing your campaign data and processes, you can identify potential issues and determine the root cause of the problem. Here are some steps you can take to find out which of the above reasons is causing your performance marketing failure:

1. Define clear goals: Start by reviewing your campaign goals and metrics to ensure they are specific, measurable, and achievable. If your goals are unclear or too broad, it can be challenging to evaluate campaign performance.
2. Check your targeting: Review your targeting settings to ensure you are reaching the right audience. Look for patterns in your audience demographics, interests, and behaviors to identify potential mismatches between your targeting and your goals.
3. Review your landing pages: Check your landing pages to see if they are optimized for conversions. Look for issues such as slow loading times, confusing navigation, or unclear calls-to-action that may be driving potential customers away.
4. Evaluate your ad creative: Review your ad creative to see if it is visually appealing and relevant to your target audience. Check for issues such as poor image quality, unclear messaging, or inconsistent branding.
5. Analyze your data: Use your data analytics tools to review your campaign data and identify patterns or trends that may be contributing to poor

performance. Look for areas of low click-through rates, high bounce rates, or low conversion rates that may indicate problems.

6. Test different variables: Experiment with different variables such as ad creative, targeting, or landing page design to see what works best for your audience. Use A/B testing or other testing methods to compare the performance of different variables and identify potential improvements.

7. Diversify your channels: Consider diversifying your channels to reach a broader audience. Experiment with different channels such as social media, search, or display advertising to see what works best for your audience.

In conclusion, by systematically reviewing your campaign data and processes, you can identify potential issues and determine the root cause of your performance marketing failure. Start by defining clear goals, checking your targeting, reviewing your landing pages and ad creative, analyzing your data, testing different variables, and diversifying your channels. By doing so, you can optimize your campaign and achieve better results.

16

Benefits of Performance Marketing

P erformance marketing is a type of marketing that focuses on driving measurable results and business outcomes, such as leads, sales, or conversions. Unlike traditional marketing, performance marketing is highly data-driven and relies on a range of digital channels, including search engine advertising, social media advertising, affiliate marketing, and email marketing.

Here are some of the benefits of performance marketing with real-world examples:

1. Measurable ROI: Performance marketing allows businesses to measure the return on investment (ROI) of their marketing efforts accurately. By tracking key performance indicators (KPIs) such as cost per lead, cost per acquisition, or customer lifetime value, businesses can determine which marketing channels and campaigns are most effective at driving revenue. For instance, Airbnb uses performance marketing to track and optimize the effectiveness of its digital ads across various channels, such as Facebook, Instagram, and Google.

2. Targeted Advertising: Performance marketing enables businesses to target their ideal audience with precision, thanks to the availability of data-driven targeting options. For example, Facebook and Instagram offer advanced targeting capabilities that allow businesses to reach spe-

cific demographics, interests, behaviors, and even lookalike audiences. By using data-driven targeting, businesses can reduce wasteful spending on irrelevant audiences and increase the chances of conversions. For instance, online retailer ASOS uses performance marketing to target its ads to specific customer segments, such as young women interested in fashion.

3. Cost-Effective: Performance marketing can be more cost-effective than traditional marketing methods because it allows businesses to pay only for the results they achieve, such as clicks, leads, or sales. This means that businesses can avoid the high upfront costs of traditional advertising, such as TV or print ads, and focus on channels that offer a higher ROI. For instance, meal kit delivery service Blue Apron uses performance marketing to drive new sign-ups and subscriptions at a cost-effective rate by partnering with influencers and running Facebook ads.

4. Scalability: Performance marketing offers scalability, allowing businesses to increase or decrease their marketing efforts based on their business needs and goals. For instance, a company might increase its marketing spend during peak sales seasons or decrease it during slow periods. This flexibility enables businesses to optimize their marketing budgets and maximize their ROI. For example, ride-hailing company Uber uses performance marketing to scale its user acquisition efforts globally, allowing it to quickly expand into new markets and grow its user base.

5. Data-Driven Optimization: Performance marketing enables businesses to collect and analyze data in real-time, allowing them to optimize their marketing campaigns continuously. By monitoring KPIs and making data-driven decisions, businesses can adjust their targeting, messaging, and creative to maximize their results. For example, online retailer Zappos uses performance marketing to test and optimize its email marketing campaigns continually, resulting in higher open rates and click-through rates.

In conclusion, performance marketing offers several benefits that can help

businesses drive results and achieve their marketing objectives. From accurate ROI tracking to targeted advertising and cost-effectiveness, performance
marketing provides businesses with the tools they need to succeed in today's
digital landscape.

17

Performance Marketing Examples

Performance marketing is a type of digital marketing that is focused on driving specific actions or conversions, such as sales, sign-ups, or downloads. The key metric of performance marketing is the return on investment (ROI), which is measured by comparing the cost of the marketing campaign to the revenue or value generated by the campaign. In this article, we will discuss some examples of performance marketing and how they can help businesses achieve their marketing goals.

1. Affiliate Marketing:

Affiliate marketing is a performance-based marketing strategy in which a business rewards affiliates for each customer or sale they bring to the business. Affiliates can promote the business's products or services through various channels such as blogs, social media, email marketing, and more. The business pays the affiliate a commission for each sale that is generated through their referral. This is a popular performance marketing strategy for e-commerce businesses, as it allows them to reach a wider audience and increase sales without spending a lot on advertising.

1. Pay-Per-Click Advertising:

Pay-per-click (PPC) advertising is a form of digital advertising in which businesses pay each time someone clicks on their ad. This type of advertising is commonly used on search engines like Google, where businesses bid on keywords related to their products or services. When someone searches for those keywords, the business's ad will appear at the top of the search results. PPC advertising is a popular performance marketing strategy because businesses only pay for the clicks they receive, which means they can target their advertising budget to specific audiences and track their ROI easily.

1. Influencer Marketing:

Influencer marketing is a performance marketing strategy in which businesses partner with social media influencers to promote their products or services. Influencers have a large following on social media platforms like Instagram, YouTube, and TikTok, and businesses can leverage this following to reach new audiences. The business pays the influencer a fee or provides them with free products in exchange for the influencer promoting their products to their followers. Influencer marketing can be highly effective for businesses that are looking to build brand awareness and reach a younger audience.

1. Email Marketing:

Email marketing is a performance marketing strategy in which businesses send promotional messages or newsletters to a list of subscribers. The goal of email marketing is to encourage subscribers to take a specific action, such as making a purchase or signing up for a free trial. Businesses can track the success of their email marketing campaigns by monitoring the open rates, click-through rates, and conversion rates of their emails. Email marketing is a cost-effective way to reach a targeted audience and can be highly effective when used in combination with other performance marketing strategies.

1. Retargeting:

Retargeting is a performance marketing strategy in which businesses show ads to people who have previously visited their website but did not make a purchase or take another desired action. Retargeting is often used in combination with other performance marketing strategies, such as PPC advertising or social media advertising, to encourage people to return to the business's website and complete a desired action. Retargeting can be highly effective for businesses that are looking to increase their conversion rates and ROI.

In conclusion, performance marketing is a powerful strategy for businesses that want to achieve specific marketing goals and track their ROI. By using a combination of performance marketing strategies, businesses can reach their target audience, increase their conversions, and ultimately grow their business.

Digital marketing charkravyuh

The term "Digital Marketing Charkravyuh" refers to a strategic framework for digital marketing that is designed to create a comprehensive and cohesive online presence. The term "Charkravyuh" is a Sanskrit word that means "maze," and it is used to describe a complex and intricate strategy that is designed to achieve a particular objective.

Digital Marketing Charkravyuh is designed to help businesses build a strong online presence that will attract customers, increase brand awareness, and drive sales. It is a multi-faceted approach that combines various digital marketing tactics to create a powerful and cohesive online strategy.

The following are the key components of Digital Marketing Charkravyuh:

1. Website Design and Development: The first step in creating a Digital Marketing Charkravyuh is to design and develop a website that is user-friendly, visually appealing, and optimized for search engines. The website should also be mobile-friendly and responsive, ensuring that it

can be accessed on any device.

2. Search Engine Optimization (SEO): SEO is a crucial component of any Digital Marketing Charkravyuh. It involves optimizing the website for search engines so that it ranks higher in search engine results pages (SERPs). This can be achieved through keyword research, on-page optimization, link building, and other techniques.

3. Pay-Per-Click Advertising (PPC): PPC advertising involves placing ads on search engine results pages or other websites and paying each time a user clicks on the ad. This can be an effective way to drive traffic to the website and increase sales.

4. Social Media Marketing: Social media marketing involves using social media platforms such as Facebook, Twitter, and Instagram to promote the business and engage with customers. This can include creating and sharing content, running ads, and responding to customer inquiries.

5. Content Marketing: Content marketing involves creating and sharing valuable content such as blog posts, videos, and infographics to attract and engage customers. This can help establish the business as a thought leader in its industry and drive traffic to the website.

6. Email Marketing: Email marketing involves sending targeted emails to customers and prospects to promote the business and drive sales. This can include newsletters, promotional emails, and abandoned cart emails.

7. Analytics and Reporting: Analytics and reporting are crucial components of any Digital Marketing Charkravyuh. This involves tracking website traffic, conversion rates, and other metrics to measure the success of the marketing strategy and make data-driven decisions.

In conclusion, Digital Marketing Charkravyuh is a comprehensive and multi-faceted approach to digital marketing that combines various tactics to create a cohesive and effective online strategy. By incorporating website design and development, SEO, PPC advertising, social media marketing, content marketing, email marketing, and analytics and reporting, businesses can build a strong online presence and drive sales.

What could break your digital marketing chakravyuh, would you need an Abhimanyu or Arjun for this?

Digital marketing Charkravyuh is a comprehensive and cohesive online marketing strategy that combines various tactics to achieve business objectives. While this approach can be effective in driving online success, there are certain factors that can break the Charkravyuh and hinder its effectiveness. Here are some steps that could break the digital marketing Charkravyuh:

1. Poor Website Design and User Experience: The website is the foundation of the digital marketing Charkravyuh, and a poorly designed website can break the entire strategy. A website that is difficult to navigate, slow to load, or not optimized for mobile devices can turn off potential customers and negatively impact search engine rankings.

2. Ineffective Search Engine Optimization (SEO): SEO is a crucial component of the digital marketing Charkravyuh, and a lack of optimization or ineffective optimization can significantly impact website visibility in search engine rankings. This can result in lower website traffic and reduced visibility to potential customers.

3. Ineffective Pay-Per-Click (PPC) Advertising: PPC advertising is an effective way to drive traffic to the website, but an ineffective PPC campaign can be a waste of resources. Ineffective targeting, ad copy, or bidding strategy can result in low conversion rates, high bounce rates, and wasted ad spend.

4. Poor Social Media Engagement: Social media marketing is a key component of the digital marketing Charkravyuh, but it requires consistent and engaging content to be effective. A lack of engagement or inconsistent posting can result in a decrease in followers, lower engagement rates, and reduced visibility.

5. Ineffective Content Marketing: Content marketing is a crucial component of the digital marketing Charkravyuh, but creating content that does not resonate with the target audience can result in low engagement rates and a lack of traffic to the website.

6. Ineffective Email Marketing: Email marketing is an effective way to nurture leads and drive sales, but ineffective targeting, poor copywriting, or a lack of personalization can result in low open rates, high unsubscribe rates, and decreased sales.

7. Lack of Analytics and Reporting: Analytics and reporting are crucial components of the digital marketing Charkravyuh, and a lack of tracking or ineffective reporting can make it difficult to measure the success of the strategy or make data-driven decisions.

In conclusion, the digital marketing Charkravyuh is a comprehensive and cohesive online marketing strategy that requires careful planning, execution, and analysis. Any one of the above factors, if not addressed or managed effectively, can break the entire Charkravyuh and hinder its effectiveness in achieving business objectives.

Skill set required to design and execute the digital marketing chakravyuh

Designing and executing a successful digital marketing Charkravyuh requires a range of skills and expertise in different areas of digital marketing. Here are some key skills that are essential for designing and executing a digital marketing Charkravyuh:

1. Strategic Thinking: The ability to think strategically and create a cohesive digital marketing plan that aligns with business objectives is crucial for designing and executing a digital marketing Charkravyuh.

2. Website Design and Development: Knowledge of website design and development is essential for creating a user-friendly and optimized website that is an integral part of the digital marketing Charkravyuh.

3. Search Engine Optimization (SEO): A strong understanding of SEO tactics, including keyword research, on-page optimization, link building, and analytics, is crucial for ensuring the website ranks high in search engine results pages (SERPs).

4. Pay-Per-Click Advertising (PPC): Expertise in PPC advertising, includ-

ing keyword research, ad copywriting, bidding strategy, and analytics, is essential for driving targeted traffic to the website and achieving business objectives.

5. Social Media Marketing: Knowledge of social media platforms, content creation, engagement strategies, and analytics is critical for engaging with customers and promoting the business through social media marketing.

6. Content Marketing: Expertise in content creation, including blog writing, video production, and infographic design, is essential for creating valuable content that attracts and engages customers.

7. Email Marketing: Knowledge of email marketing tactics, including list segmentation, copywriting, personalization, automation, and analytics, is crucial for nurturing leads and driving sales.

8. Analytics and Reporting: Proficiency in analytics and reporting tools, including Google Analytics, SEMRush, and Moz, is critical for tracking website traffic, conversion rates, and other metrics to measure the success of the digital marketing Charkravyuh and make data-driven decisions.

In conclusion, designing and executing a digital marketing Charkravyuh requires a diverse skill set that spans various areas of digital marketing. Strategic thinking, website design and development, SEO, PPC advertising, social media marketing, content marketing, email marketing, and analytics and reporting are all essential skills for creating a successful digital marketing strategy.

How do I know all this and who am I?

Krishna Mohan Avancha is an Indian author and digital marketing expert with extensive experience in lead generation, SEO (Search Engine Optimization), SEM (Search Engine Marketing), and other related fields. He has worked in the industry for several years and has helped many businesses achieve their marketing goals.

Krishna Mohan Avancha is the author of the book "Digital Marketing: A Practical Approach," which provides a comprehensive overview of the digital marketing landscape and offers practical tips for businesses looking to improve their online presence. The book covers topics such as SEO, SEM, social media marketing, email marketing, content marketing, and more.

In addition to his work as an author, Krishna Mohan Avancha has also worked as a digital marketing consultant and has helped many businesses improve their online visibility and generate more leads. He has a deep understanding of the latest digital marketing trends and best practices, and is known for his ability to create effective marketing strategies that deliver results.

Overall, Krishna Mohan Avancha is a highly respected figure in the Indian digital marketing industry, and his expertise and insights have helped many businesses achieve success online.

Krishna mohan avancha books

Krishna Mohan Avancha is an Indian author who has written several books on digital marketing, lead generation, and related topics. His books are highly regarded in the industry and are widely read by marketing professionals, entrepreneurs, and business owners.

One of Krishna Mohan Avancha's most popular books is "Digital Marketing: A Practical Approach," which provides a comprehensive overview of the digital marketing landscape and offers practical tips for businesses looking to improve their online presence. The book covers topics such as SEO, SEM, social media marketing, email marketing, content marketing, and more. It is written in a clear and concise manner, making it accessible to readers of all levels of expertise.

Another popular book by Krishna Mohan Avancha is "Lead Generation Techniques: A Beginner's Guide to Generating High-Quality Leads," which focuses on the crucial process of lead generation in marketing. The book provides an overview of different lead generation techniques, including SEO, content marketing, social media marketing, email marketing, and more. It also includes practical tips and strategies for businesses looking to generate more leads and convert them into paying customers.

Krishna Mohan Avancha has also written several other books on topics such as SEO, SEM, and social media marketing. These books are designed to provide readers with a deep understanding of these important marketing channels and how they can be leveraged to improve business results.

What sets Krishna Mohan Avancha's books apart is their practicality and applicability to real-world business situations. Rather than focusing on abstract theories and concepts, his books provide actionable advice that businesses can implement immediately to improve their marketing results.

Overall, Krishna Mohan Avancha's books are highly recommended for anyone looking to improve their digital marketing knowledge and skills. Whether you're a marketing professional or a business owner, his books provide valuable insights and practical strategies that can help you achieve your marketing goals.

Some of his other popular works are as follows:

ABM Marketing Secretts Unveiled: The Secretts Unveiled: Series: Book 9:

'ABM is all about building better quality relationships, the ROI will follow' - Andy Bacon, B2B Marketing quotes explains all that this book holds. This book can be used as your go-to-guide to build long-lasting relationships with your customers where if you want you could read and figure out more ways than I have described to get International customers or quick conversions by simply following this book step-by-step. I am proud to present this comprehensive journal of my own steps which I have used to implement over 7 full-cycle ABM implementations from strategy to fruit-bearing in the organizations that I have worked. This book is a short synopsis in its best form possible.

Undisputed!!!: Google Ranking in a month!!!

Though there is no guaranteed way to quickly achieve a top ranking on Google, as the search algorithm is constantly changing and there are many factors that determine a website's ranking. The only way to get the results for your brand lies in Integrated with guerrilla marketing techniques where you could focus on hedgehog technique to begin with niche but focused keywords and grow locally before taking on the big players in your field. However, some strategies to improve your website's ranking include:

Optimizing your website's content for search engines by including relevant keywords
   Building high-quality back links to your website from other reputable sites
   Ensuring that your website is mobile-friendly and loads quickly
   Submitting your website to Google's Search Console and regularly monitoring your website's performance
   It's important to note that achieving a high ranking on Google takes time and effort, and shouldn't be viewed as a short-term solution.

All Hail, the Marketing Wizards!: The Complete Beginner's Guide to Digital Marketing Strategies

WARNING: Do Not Read This Book If You Hate it when a plan comes together

To build a successful business, you need to stop doing random acts of marketing/push strategy and start following a reliable plan for rapid, consistent, and easily sustainable business growth. Traditionally, creating a marketing plan has always been a difficult and time-consuming process, which is why it often doesn't get done.

With this book, I present to you my 15 years of experience in a condensed and concise format. Some of the most notable points covered in this book are:

- How to get new customers, clients, or followers and how to make more profit from existing ones.
- How to close sales without being pushy, needy, or obnoxious while turning the tables and having prospects begging you to take their money.
- How to annihilate competitors and make yourself the only logical choice.
- How to charge high prices for your products and services and have customers actually thank you for it.

Empathy Marketing!

Empathy is the key to unlocking the hearts and minds of your customers. And in today's hyper-connected world, it's more important than ever to build deep, emotional connections with your target audience. That's where the Empathy Marketing book comes in.

This groundbreaking guide is packed with insights, strategies, and practical tips for creating more empathetic marketing campaigns. You'll learn how to tap into the psychology of empathy to better understand your customers' needs, pain points, and aspirations. You'll

74

discover how to craft messaging and experiences that truly resonate with your audience, using language, imagery, and design that speaks directly to their emotions.

But the Empathy Marketing book isn't just about theory – it's also about action. You'll get step-by-step guidance on how to implement empathy marketing in your own campaigns, with real-world examples and case studies that show you how other brands have successfully used this approach. Whether you're a seasoned marketer or just starting out, this book will give you the tools and confidence you need to take your marketing to the next level.

But don't just take our word for it. Here's what some early readers have said about the Empathy Marketing book:

"This book is a game-changer for anyone who wants to connect with customers on a deeper level. The strategies and tactics are easy to implement, and the results speak for themselves." - Jane Smith, Marketing Director

"I've been in marketing for 20 years, and this is the most refreshing and insightful book I've read in a long time. It's a must-read for anyone who wants to stay ahead of the curve." - John Doe, Chief Marketing Officer

So whether you're looking to build brand loyalty, increase conversions, or simply make a positive impact on the world, the Empathy Marketing book is the ultimate guide to achieving your goals. Get your copy today and start connecting with your customers in a whole new way.

Dominate Your Real Estate Market: Proven Lead Generation Techniques for Explosive Growth (The Secretts Unveiled Book 10)

Are you tired of struggling to get ahead in the competitive world of real estate? Do you want to become the go-to agent in your market and achieve explosive growth in your business? Look no further than "How to Dominate Your Real Estate Market."

This comprehensive guide is packed with proven lead generation techniques that will help you stand out from the competition and attract more clients than ever before. You'll learn how to leverage the latest technology and marketing strategies to build a strong brand, generate quality leads, and close more deals.

Inside, you'll discover:

The secrets to building a powerful personal brand that resonates with your target market

How to create a lead generation machine that consistently delivers high-quality leads

Advanced marketing strategies to help you reach more clients and close more deals

The importance of building strong relationships with your clients and how to do it effectively

And much more!

Whether you're a seasoned agent or just starting out in the real estate industry, "How to Dominate Your Real Estate Market" will give you the tools and strategies you need to achieve explosive growth and become the top agent in your market. Don't wait - get your copy today and start dominating your real estate market!

Lead Games: Game For Lead Generation!

Leave behind the conundrum of lead generation strategist telling you their ways which may or may not work and grab a copy of this single book which gives you the full blown scale of what one needs to be done to get leads from the different properties that you have. This book can get your business organic leads for life! In this book you will discover:How Search Engine Optimization can get you leadsHow Pay Per Click Advertising can get you leadsHow Lead Generating Website can get you leadsHow Online Networking can get you leadsHow Webinars can get you leadsHow Industry Research Reports can get you leadsHow Online Marketing Videos can get you leadsHow White Papers or e-Books can get you leadsHow E-newsletter can get you leadsHow Blogging can get you leads

18

Extra Material for getting started or to get the best of performance marketing results

- **Ad Copy Template:**

[Headline]: Grab the user's attention with a catchy headline that highlights the main benefit of your product/service. [Description]: Provide a brief description of what you are offering and what makes it unique. [Call-to-action]: Include a clear call-to-action that encourages users to take action, such as "Click Here," "Buy Now," or "Sign Up."

Version A: "Boost your productivity and streamline your workflow with our SaaS solution. Sign up now for a free trial!"

Version B: "Tired of wasting time on tedious tasks? Our SaaS solution can help. Try it now for free and experience the difference."

Version A: "Experience the power of our SaaS solution for yourself. Sign up for a free demo today!"

Version B: "Unlock the full potential of your business with our SaaS solution. Request a free demo now."

Version A: "Don't settle for inefficiency. Our SaaS solution can help you save time and get more done. Try it now!"

Version B: "Ready to take your business to the next level? Our SaaS solution can help. Sign up for a free trial today."

- **Landing Page Template:**

[Headline]: Make sure the headline on your landing page matches the ad copy. [Hero Image]: Include an eye-catching image that visually represents your product/service. [Product Description]: Provide a clear and concise description of what you are offering and its main benefits. [Testimonials]: Include testimonials from satisfied customers to build trust. [Call-to-action]: Use a prominent call-to-action button that encourages users to take action.

Landing Page A: Headline: Transform Your Business with our Powerful SaaS Solution Subheadline: Get More Sales and Boost Your Revenue with our Cutting-Edge Technology Body Copy: Our innovative SaaS solution is designed to streamline your business processes, improve customer engagement, and increase sales. With our easy-to-use platform, you can manage your sales pipeline, track customer interactions, and generate detailed reports to help you make data-driven decisions. Say goodbye to manual processes and hello to automated efficiency with our powerful software. Try it out today and start seeing results!

Call-to-Action: Sign Up for a Free Trial Now

Landing Page B: Headline: Say Hello to Your New Sales Machine Subheadline: Power Up Your Sales with our Revolutionary SaaS Solution Body Copy: Our SaaS solution is the ultimate tool for boosting your sales and taking your business to the next level. Our software is designed to automate your sales process, from lead generation to deal closure, so you can focus on what matters most – growing your business. Our powerful platform includes advanced analytics and reporting tools to help you make data-driven decisions, and our easy-to-use interface means you can start seeing results right away. Say goodbye to manual sales processes and hello to your new sales machine. Try it out today!

Call-to-Action: Start Your Free Trial Now

- **Email Template:**

[Subject Line]: Grab the user's attention with a catchy subject line that entices them to open the email. [Introduction]: Start with a friendly greeting and a brief introduction. [Value Proposition]: Highlight the main benefit of your product/service and explain why it's valuable to the user. [Product/Service Description]: Provide a detailed description of what you are offering and how it can solve the user's problem. [Testimonials]: Include testimonials from satisfied customers to build trust. [Call-to-action]: Use a prominent call-to-action button that encourages users to take action.

Email Sample A:
  Subject Line: Introducing [Product Name] - [Benefit]
  Dear [Recipient],
  Are you tired of [pain point]? Do you want to [benefit]? Look no further than [Product Name].
  Our SaaS product is designed to [benefit] while solving the problems of [pain point]. With [Product Name], you'll be able to [unique feature] and [unique feature], all while streamlining your workflow.
  Don't just take our word for it - see what our satisfied customers have to say about their experience with [Product Name]: [Customer testimonial].
  Ready to experience the benefits of [Product Name] for yourself? Get started today by signing up for a free trial!
  Best regards, [Your Name]
  Email Sample B:
  Subject Line: Don't Miss Out on [Benefit] - Try [Product Name] Today
  Dear [Recipient],
  As a [profession/industry], you know how important it is to [pain point]. But what if you could [benefit] while doing so more efficiently and effectively?
  Introducing [Product Name] - the SaaS product designed to do just that. With [Product Name], you'll be able to [unique feature] and [unique feature], all while streamlining your workflow and boosting your productivity.
  But don't just take our word for it - try [Product Name] for yourself with a

free trial. You have nothing to lose and everything to gain.

Start experiencing the benefits of [Product Name] today and see the difference it can make for your [profession/industry].

Best regards, [Your Name]

- **Social Media Ad Template:**

[Headline]: Grab the user's attention with a catchy headline that highlights the main benefit of your product/service. [Visual Content]: Use high-quality images or videos that are visually appealing and represent your product/service. [Product/Service Description]: Provide a clear and concise description of what you are offering and its main benefits. [Call-to-action]: Include a clear call-to-action that encourages users to take action, such as "Click Here," "Buy Now," or "Sign Up."

Social Media Ad Template A:

Headline: [Product Name] - The Solution to Your [Pain Point]

Body Text: Say goodbye to [pain point] and hello to [benefit] with [Product Name]. Our SaaS product is designed to [unique feature] and [unique feature], making your workflow smoother and more efficient than ever before.

Don't just take our word for it - see what our satisfied customers have to say about their experience with [Product Name]: [Customer testimonial].

Ready to experience the benefits of [Product Name] for yourself? Sign up for a free trial today and see the difference it can make for your [profession/industry].

CTA: Sign up for a free trial

Social Media Ad Template B:

Headline: Boost Your [Profession/Industry] Productivity with [Product Name]

Body Text: As a [profession/industry], you know how important it is to [pain point]. But what if you could do so while boosting your productivity and streamlining your workflow?

Introducing [Product Name] - the SaaS product designed specifically for [profession/industry]. With [Product Name], you'll be able to [unique feature] and [unique feature], all while saving time and achieving better results.

Ready to see the difference [Product Name] can make for your [profession/industry]? Sign up for a free trial today and experience the benefits for yourself.

CTA: Sign up for a free trial

- **Telecalling script**

Script 1:
Hello, [Prospect Name], this is [Your Name] from [Your Company]. I hope you're doing well.

I'm calling to introduce you to our SaaS solution that can help your business achieve its goals more efficiently. We specialize in [Briefly describe the key features and benefits of your SaaS solution].

Our clients have seen a significant increase in productivity and ROI by using our SaaS solution, and I believe it can do the same for your business.

I would love to schedule a demo to show you how our SaaS solution works and answer any questions you may have. Would you be interested in scheduling a demo?

[If they express interest, you can provide some more details about the demo, such as its duration and what they can expect to learn. You can also offer to send more information via email.]

[If they're hesitant, try to address their concerns and offer some more information about your solution. You can also offer to schedule a follow-up call or send some more information to help them make a decision.]

[If they agree to the demo, schedule a date and time that works for both of you and confirm the details.]

Thank you for your time, and I look forward to speaking with you soon.

Script 2:
Hello, [Prospect Name], this is [Your Name] from [Your Company]. I hope I'm not interrupting anything important.

I wanted to talk to you about how our SaaS solution can help your business improve its efficiency and productivity. Our solution is designed to [Briefly describe the key features and benefits of your SaaS solution].

Many of our clients have seen a significant increase in their revenue and productivity by using our solution. I would love to schedule a demo to show you how it works and answer any questions you may have. Would you be interested in scheduling a demo?

[If they're hesitant, try to address their concerns and provide some more information about your solution. You can also offer to schedule a follow-up call or send some more information to help them make a decision.]

[If they agree to the demo, schedule a date and time that works for both of you and confirm the details.]

Thank you for your time, and I look forward to speaking with you soon.

Script 3:

Hello, [Prospect Name], this is [Your Name] from [Your Company]. I hope you're having a great day.

I wanted to discuss how our SaaS solution can help your business achieve its goals more efficiently. Our solution is designed to [Briefly describe the key features and benefits of your SaaS solution].

We have a special offer for new clients where you can [Describe any promotions or discounts that you're offering]. I would love to schedule a demo to show you how our solution works and answer any questions you may have. Would you be interested in scheduling a demo?

[If they're hesitant, try to address their concerns and provide some more information about your solution. You can also offer to schedule a follow-up call or send some more information to help them make a decision.]

[If they agree to the demo, schedule a date and time that works for both of you and confirm the details.]

Thank you for your time, and I look forward to speaking with you soon.

- **Whatsapp Script for performance marketing:**

Message 1: Hi [Prospect Name], this is [Your Name] from [Your Company]. I hope this message finds you well. I wanted to reach out and introduce you to our SaaS solution that can help your business improve its efficiency and productivity. Our solution is designed to [Briefly describe the key features and benefits of your SaaS solution].

Message 2 (sent 2-3 days after Message 1): Hi [Prospect Name], I wanted to follow up and see if you had any questions or concerns about our SaaS solution. Our solution can help your business achieve its goals more efficiently, and I would love to schedule a demo to show you how it works. Would you be interested in scheduling a demo?

Message 3 (sent 2-3 days after Message 2): Hi [Prospect Name], I hope you're doing well. I wanted to remind you about our SaaS solution that can help your business achieve its goals more efficiently. Our clients have seen a significant increase in productivity and ROI by using our solution, and I believe it can do the same for your business. Would you like to schedule a demo to learn more?

Message 4 (sent 2-3 days after Message 3): Hi [Prospect Name], this is [Your Name] from [Your Company]. I hope everything is going well. I wanted to check in one last time and see if you had any questions or concerns about our SaaS solution. If you're interested in learning more, we would love to schedule a demo and show you how our solution can benefit your business. Please let me know if you're interested.

Note: It's important to personalize the messages and adjust the frequency of the messages based on your prospect's response. If they show interest, you can schedule a demo right away. If they don't respond, you may want to wait a few more days before sending another message or try a different approach.

- **Video Script for boosting SaaS Product Sales:**

Title: Boost Your Productivity with [SaaS Product Name]: A Complete Review

Introduction: Hello and welcome to our channel! In today's video, we will be reviewing [SaaS product name], a revolutionary software designed to boost productivity and help businesses grow. With this software, you can streamline your workflow, automate your tasks, and get more done in less time. So, if you're looking for a tool to enhance your productivity, then stick around till the end of the video.

Section 1: Problem Identification Are you tired of spending countless hours on repetitive tasks, like data entry or scheduling appointments? Do you find it challenging to manage your team's workload and ensure everyone is on the same page? Well, you're not alone. Many businesses struggle with these productivity issues, which can significantly impact their bottom line.

Section 2: Solution Presentation That's where [SaaS product name] comes in. This software offers a suite of tools that can help you automate your workflows, manage your team, and increase productivity. With [SaaS product name], you can:

- Automate repetitive tasks: [SaaS product name] offers a range of automation tools that can help you save time and reduce errors. For example, you can set up automated workflows for data entry, email marketing, or social media posting.
- Streamline your communication: [SaaS product name] offers a built-in chat feature that allows you to communicate with your team in real-time. You can also assign tasks and track progress, ensuring everyone is on the same page.
- Track your progress: With [SaaS product name], you can track your team's progress and identify areas for improvement. You can generate reports and analyze data to make informed decisions and optimize your workflow.

Section 3: Benefits and Features

- User-friendly interface: [SaaS product name] has a simple and intuitive interface that makes it easy for anyone to use, regardless of their technical expertise.
- Cloud-based: [SaaS product name] is cloud-based, which means you can access it from anywhere, at any time. All you need is an internet connection and a device.
- Customizable: [SaaS product name] is highly customizable, allowing you to tailor it to your specific needs. You can create custom workflows, set up automated tasks, and configure settings to suit your business requirements.

Section 4: Social Proof But don't just take our word for it. [SaaS product name] has helped hundreds of businesses increase their productivity and grow their revenue. Here are some testimonials from our satisfied customers:

[Include 2-3 customer testimonials here]

Section 5: Call to Action So, what are you waiting for? If you're ready to boost your productivity and take your business to the next level, then head over to our website and sign up for [SaaS product name] today. We offer a free trial, so you can try it out risk-free and see the benefits for yourself.

Conclusion: That's it for today's video. We hope you found this review helpful and informative. If you have any questions or comments, please leave them down below, and we'll be sure to get back to you. Thanks for watching, and we'll see you in the next video!

Short #1: Problem-Solution

[Video shows a person struggling with a common problem that your SaaS product solves]

Voiceover: Are you tired of [common problem]? [Person sighs or shakes head] You're not alone. [Statistics appear on screen to emphasize the prevalence of the problem]. But what if I told you there was an easy solution? [Product name] is a SaaS product that [explains how the product solves the problem]. [Video shows the person using the product and experiencing relief]. Say goodbye to [problem] and hello to [benefit of using the product]. Try [product name] today.

Short #2: Testimonial

[Video shows a person using your SaaS product and talking about their positive experience]

Person: Hi, I'm [Name], and I just wanted to share my experience using [product name]. I was struggling with [problem the product solves] and nothing seemed to work. But then I tried [product name] and it's been a game changer. [Person explains how the product has helped them and highlights any unique features or benefits]. If you're struggling with [same problem], I highly recommend giving [product name] a try.

Short #3: How-To

[Video shows a quick tutorial on how to use your SaaS product]

Voiceover: Are you curious about how [product name] works? Let me show you. [Video shows a screen recording of the product being used and any unique or noteworthy features are highlighted with text or a voiceover]. It's that simple. [Call-to-action] Try [product name] today and see how it can help streamline your [relevant task or process].

These templates can be customized and adapted to fit your specific business and audience. Remember to track and measure your performance marketing campaigns to continuously improve and optimize your results.